CONVERSATIONS WITH COVEY

BRIAN COVEY

ISBN: 978-1-64184-518-2 Hardback
ISBN: 978-1-64184-519-9 Paperback
ISBN: 978-1-64184-520-5 Ebook

TABLE OF CONTENTS

INTRODUCTION

"Ever since I was a child I have had this instinctive urge for expansion and growth. To me, the function and duty of a quality human being is the sincere and honest development of one's potential."

— Bruce Lee

Growing up in Memphis, TN my love for the sport of soccer led me to the opportunity to travel the world, compete at the highest levels, and experience all the great challenges that have shaped me into the husband, dad, and leader I am today.

Today, I'm a Vice President in the mortgage industry with loanDepot, one of the top 5 lenders in the nation. I'm still very passionate about being part of a championship team and equipping our team with the tools to excel, leadership development, and leading change in our industry.

I started the Brian Covey Show podcast in 2020 as a way to connect with amazing people in my network to share their stories of overcoming adversity, setbacks, and challenges. The guests on my show were intentionally chosen because of their diverse backgrounds. None of them came into the business world with superpowers or anything inaccessible to the everyday person, but they did have a special passion, to learn and grow. That's why you are here too because you also have that passion.

In this book, I will be highlighting some of my favorite guests from my podcast and I might even throw in some of my own knowledge and skills I've learned throughout my experiences. Each chapter is packed with inspiration, hope & actionable steps to help you win your game of life no matter where you are.

Chapter 1
Brittany Hodak

W hat I loved about interviewing Brittany is her focus on creating superfans. You'll hear about that in a moment. I also admired how she used the platform she was given on *Shark Tank* to launch her brand, business, and mission.

Since our conversation, I've made it a point to identify and build out my "Superfans." Just that one little shift has lit a new fire under my business and my broader mission to get inspiring, hope-filled messages out to people like you.

As you're taking in Brittany's wisdom below, let her insights on building your loyal followers and leveraging the platforms you're given, big or small, set you on a path for massive success. Enjoy!

Building a Superfan

What is a Superfan? Brittany Hodak founded, and subsequently exited, a business called The Superfan Company that creates collectible items for fans of music artists, sports teams, movies, and basically anything that people can be fans of. The Superfan Company became a million-dollar company in its first year, and the success is highly contributed from Brittany's insightful way of conducting business. She created her own fanbase out of the people that she did business with, and we call that... building superfans.

The secret to creating superfans, Brittany says, is connecting your story to their story. Connecting your story to your customer story that overlaps is the superfan zone, and that's where superfandom happens. What a lot of people get wrong, is they don't listen. They just simply don't listen to the customers either because they are so focused on showing what they know or thinking they know that the best thing to do is for me to say these things or to go through the script. We can get stuck in these cycles. You've got to develop a set of critical questions that are going to help you understand what the person's needs are. If you don't connect your story to their story, they're absolutely going to forget you and just become another person.

When Brittany teaches about superfandom she likes to tell people to start with their story. She'll ask them to tell me why they're the very best person in their market for someone to work with, and they either can't answer it or they default to something about their company. Then her response is "No no no, don't tell me about your company first. A customer doesn't work with a company. A customer works with a human, and I want to know as a human, why are you the very best person in your market to help people?" People can't always answer that question, and her thought is that if you can't answer that question, how could you expect a customer to answer that question?

If it's not obvious why you're the best, then the logical conclusion that somebody's going to come to is that you must not be. You must not be the best, or we would know why you were the best. Learning how to do a better job of listening to uncover important details, because no two customers are ever going to be the same.

People forget that the absolute cheapest way to acquire a customer, no matter what business you're in, is through referrals. Using mortgage as an example, if the first time somebody who you help to get a mortgage is hearing from you again is because you pick up the phone and say like, "Hey, do you want to refinance?", what kind of experience is that? Is that someone who is going to be primed to create more customers for you? There's a quote that Brittany read several years ago, that really changed the way she thought about marketing. The quote is "The purpose of a business is to create a customer who creates customers." If you can do that, if every customer you create is creating more customers for you, then that really is superfandom in a nutshell.

THE RIGHT QUESTION IS WHO?

One thing that Brittany thinks people get tripped up with, especially around the idea of video, is people get really, really hung up on the how. They say I don't know how to use TikTok, I don't know how to use Instagram, or I don't know how to do email marketing. **If your first question that you're asking is 'how', you're going to fail.** If you're not super clear on who you're trying to reach, who your exact customer is, then you're never going to get it right with the how. The who is infinitely more important than the how because the how is always going to be changing.

If you're not super clear on who you are trying to serve, and why you're the best person to serve them, it's always just going to seem desperate. That's a strong word, but it's the word that comes to mind when I see a TikTok video of a 50-year-old. How is that serving your customer? How is this making someone think you are the right person to help them with what they need, and not just some desperate attempt to try to go viral? When seeing attempts like that that are not based on any underlying strategy, it just looks like someone who needs affirmation from strangers, which isn't going to be the trait at the top of the list when you're looking for an expert to help you.

THE PLATINUM RULE

You have to create a connection in a way that's authentic to you. It's got to be authentic both to your story and your customer's story. The Platinum Rule, coined by Dr. Tony Alessandra, is one of Brittany's favorites. We all grew up with the golden rule, which is to treat others the way you want to be treated, but the Platinum Rule says, treat others the way *they* want to be treated. It's so much more powerful because it's coming from a place of understanding that not everyone wants the same things that you want. Not everybody has the same life experiences and backgrounds and preferences. For example, picking up the phone is great, unless you've got a customer who doesn't like to talk on the phone. In that case, it's not picking up the phone, it's sending them a message, handwritten note, or whatever their communication preference is.

It is so easy, now we've got so many powerful tools at our fingertips, we just have to take the time to automate them. So think about what it is that gives you a unique opportunity to reach out based on the intersection of your brand and your customers' brand. You know, maybe it's the kid's birthdays, maybe it's the anniversaries. Anytime someone says something to you, that you think is going to give you an opportunity to reach out again, maybe it's their favorite sports team, maybe it's the first concert they saw when they were a kid, add that as a field to your CRM, and make it your goal to get the answer to that question at some point during the first few conversations.

One tactic that Brittany uses a lot is the first concert that you went to because we all have fun memories around the concert that we went to. That brings it back to that experience of that band for them, whether it's, you're getting them tickets to a show, whether you're framing a cool vintage album cover that you found on Etsy, whatever it is, there are a million things that you can do. It's the same in our everyday lives. If you think about the most meaningful gifts you've ever received in your lifetime, they're meaningful because of the thought behind them.

It's so easy to bring up in conversation. Brittany recommends always trying to have a setlist. Try to have your setlist the way a cover band would if they're going to play at a bar. They don't just show up with one setlist, right. They've got a bunch of songs in the repertoire that they know that they can shift and move with, and every show might be different based on the audience at the bar, the environment of the bar. So having in your repertoire, here are 20 things and my goal is to get the six that make the most sense for this customer. Then follow up on a regular basis with at least one of them. Another thing Brittany does is sends people half birthday cards. Everyone gets birthday cards in the mail, but if you know someone's birthday, you know their half birthday. So when a really fun half birthday card shows up to somebody in the mail it gets their attention. You're setting yourself apart

INCORPORATE WAVE INTO YOUR COMPANY

A tool that will help you lead your company to always be creating Superfans is WAVE. WAVE is an acronym that Brittany came up with, that involves Maslow's hierarchy of needs.

For anyone not familiar, Maslow's hierarchy of needs is the concept of satisfying the base needs before you can get to the higher needs. People aren't worried about their higher needs until their basic needs are met. It's the same thing when you're talking about a brand. When you're introducing new customers or fans into your fold. So WAVE is an acronym that stands for Welcomed, Appreciated, Validated, and Engaged.

The very first step is making someone feel welcomed by your brand. A lot of times, this is going to either happen or not happen long before you ever talk to that person. Many people in sales think the relationship starts the first time they talk to the person on the phone, when they're meeting them in person, or when they exchange the first email. It's actually way before that because what you don't know is you could have lost countless leads before you ever got to that point. Maybe somebody was turned off by something that they saw on one of your personal social accounts, by the reputation that you have, or by something that they were told by somebody else when they were asking for a referral. So this is the idea of making people feel welcomed. Saying I want to work with you, I want to be here for you. It's important to not skip this step.

KNOW YOUR STORY

To connect your story to your customer's story, you first have to know your story. This story has to be specific to you because like we said before, a customer doesn't work with a company. A customer works with a human. You can start by asking yourself some simple questions to pinpoint what your personal story is:

Why are you the very best person to work with in your market?

Why do you want to be the best person in your market?

What makes you different from the other people in your market?

How do you want your clients/customers to feel when interacting with you?

How do you overcome obstacles in your market?

Who are you trying to serve?

BE MINDFUL & AUTHENTIC

Creating a company's influence starts with one person. Thoughts become words, words become actions, the action becomes reality, and we just forget the idea that one person really can change the world. One person really can make a difference. One thing to keep in mind is every interaction you have throughout the day is going to be either a Net Neutral, which will leave them feeling the exact same, a Net Negative, which means they walk away feeling worse than they did, or a Net Positive, where they feel better about themselves after the interaction.

If you stay mindful and authentic, it's possible to make every interaction you have with somebody a Net Positive for them. It then creates little ripples. You never know, if the person that you're talking to is one little step away from a breakdown. Your company needs to find its own story, but part of everyone's story should include being kind people. That is how you create Superfans.

THE SUPERFAN COMPANY

In 2014, Brittany and her cofounder were scouted to be on the television show, *Shark Tank*. They got very lucky that they were in the episode they were because it was one of the highest-rated episodes of the season. It was a lead-in for this 2020 special that there was a ton of press around. Their episode would air every couple of weeks in over 100 countries around the world. So, there is always someone seeing it for the first time. Brittany gets emails every single week, still, from people all over the world who are seeing it for the first time, even though it's been more than six years since the episode debuted.

By creating and building The Superfan Company, Brittany found her passion. She found that the most enjoyable part of being a business owner for her was the growing aspect. With a Master's in Marketing, she has always loved that side of it. Now she helps build other companies by speaking at events and consulting with businesses and personal brands.

Want to hear the full conversation, head on over to https://www.thebriancoveyshow.com/

Chapter 2
RAUL VILLACIS

Raul Villacis has a very inspiring story that I believe you need to hear. Raul is in the real estate field and spoke with me about finding leverage and having faith over fear. During the pandemic, Raul's family got sick and had to quarantine. When he started to feel better, he had a moment of realization that God is in control, not him. We're always being molded and shaped in every moment and although we convince ourselves we have full control over our lives, we actually are never in control. We need to have faith and be willing to let ourselves leverage out the responsibilities we have in our personal lives and as leaders.

When Raul's wife started to have some complications with the illness, his faith came in even stronger. This nerve-wracking time tested his faith and I think we all have experienced times that make us step back and analyze our lives as a whole. These times make us ask ourselves what are we doing? And why are we doing it? Do we have a purpose? We take for granted being alive, but if you are alive what are you going to do about it? Raul wants to make his life meaningful and impact others. I think that is a strong message that we can all learn from and use in our own lives.

DISCOVERING WEAKNESSES

Raul started off by stating that his content is not for everyone. He said, "half of the people hate me, and the other half, they get it, they love me." When he decided to train businessmen and entrepreneurs, he wanted to talk to the entrepreneur that has been through a tunnel. He wanted to talk to a certain type of individual. Raul had a very successful business, in a real estate company at an investment firm on a real estate brokerage, we did a lot of flips. It was very successful, but Raul said he "wasn't fulfilled, even though I was making a lot of money and had a team." He survived in 2008 and invested in distressed assets. He told me that he was lucky enough to find that part of the industry. Towards 2013, when they were going to start getting the peak he had this crazy idea to put together a mastermind and they did it in Vegas. They got investors, managers, real estate guys, and personal development guys.

Raul's intention at that moment wasn't for him to coach them or be the leader. It was more for him to be the curator because that's what he saw as his place at that moment. He wanted to be the curator. He had a bunch of speakers, come in and speak, but something interesting happened in that first event. When Raul got up on stage, he had a breakthrough. He felt that he wasn't being authentic, that he wasn't really sharing his true message. So when he owned his true message, he realized what he'd actually been going through. He was drinking every single day because, went through depression, anxiety, fear, and all those patterns. The reason he was able to break through is that every single person that will connect to that message will connect to my story. That's when he realized that he truly wanted to bring a message to the world and to men that it's okay for you to feel pain. It is okay for you to feel like you're failing. Now is not the time for us to pretend that we are Superman. Now it's not the time for us to pretend that we have it all together. Now is the time for us to take inventory and ask ourselves what our weaknesses are.

The Process Of Failure

As Raul looked back on the 2008 market crash, and where he failed to actually see it, he explained that the first step he went through was denial. He thought *Oh, it's not gonna happen to me. I'm stronger than this. It's not gonna affect me. I'm gonna weather the storm.* He said, "I was in denial." During that time, we felt like we couldn't do any business. We couldn't sell because there was no money being traded. Nobody was lending, the credit shrunk.

Then the second step that he went through was to pretend that he knew what he was doing. That's the mistake that he didn't adapt soon enough. By that time he knew he had to come clean to his wife that he couldn't pay the mortgage. He knew he had to come clean with all his employees and let them know that he had to let them go. He felt like a failure, and he didn't want his family and friends to know. At that point, he realized that he could have saved the business if he had adapted to the changes sooner. In a training class that Raul leads, he explains that as men we are trained to avoid pain at all costs. And because we have been trained to avoid pain, we don't know how to handle pain. We don't know how to manage failure. Therefore, we just pretend that we're strong enough to handle it.

The third step he went through was confronting his family and employees with the truth. He knew he had to stop pretending that he had everything under control. The moment he got real with himself, with his wife, and the people around him the energy started to shift away from the guilt and the shame. Now the opportunities could show up. Before he was blocked. When you are in denial and playing pretend, you're blocked. Just acknowledging that you don't know what to do and that you did fail brings you a sense of certainty. Acknowledging the pain and shame lessens the power that the pain and shame have over us.

FAITH OVER FEAR

As so many of us didn't really know what to think or believe about the pandemic, Raul thought he didn't have to worry about it. He's a strong young person and there was a lot of talk going around that it was only affecting older people. So when it hit him, it was a reality check. One second he was fine, and the next his throat was hurting and he had a high fever. It just went down the hill fast to the point that he couldn't even get up from the bed. It humbled him. Raul told me that he had never been closer to God than he is now. He never prayed. First, he got sick, and then his wife got sick. Then his biggest fear was his kids getting sick. He ended up quarantining by himself in their guest bedroom, his wife was in the master bedroom, and his kids pretty much took care of themselves for two weeks. They are teenagers, so his mother went shopping for them for groceries. When he started to get his energy back, he had his greatest breakthrough.

That's when he started to realize that we're not in control and that God is always molding and shaping us. That's when the work began. That is when his wife started to have complications. He was afraid, living in fear. But you can't live in fear and have faith. It's one or the other. You can't do both. You either have faith or you have fear. So that really tested his faith. He told me he remembers talking to God while he was sick and asking God to heal him. Raul said "I don't know if it's a fever, the voice of God saying, 'Why do you want to live? Why should I spare you?' But I felt the need to convince God, I have a purpose." That's when he thought to himself *I'm gonna do this, I'm gonna have an impact.* The point of Raul's message of faith over fear is that we take for granted being alive.

INTEGRATING

We lose sight of what is important. Your relationship with God is important. Your relationship with your family is important. Your business is important as well because you have to pay the bills, but we're not designed to work towards just one side of our lives. For Raul, the quarantine came, and he wasn't able to make any money. Now what? For instance, you focus completely on work, but a worldwide pandemic happens and you're no longer able to work as you were. Now you're at home facing your wife that you probably haven't talked to in years, facing your kids that you don't have a relationship because you don't talk to them, you're overweight, and you just don't know what to do with yourself. That's when the pressure hits. That's what happened to Raul. He realized he had everything. The money, the wife, the kids, but he was depressed because he only put his focus in one thing. He left everything else as a second, third or fourth place priority. He didn't have any integration plan. For Raul, it's important to teach men how to create integration.

TWO WAYS TO INTEGRATE:

Build a community. Have a network of like-minded people who you can help and who can help you. Raul told me "This is not the Raul Show, I'm not trying to be the next Tony Robbins, I'm actually building a community of entrepreneurs that actually care about themselves enough to actually help each other when we have those moments of hardship." In the moments when we need to level up, it makes all the difference in the world to have a group of people who will support you. You can build this group through work, school, church, sports, a friend group, or a mastermind group. But have these people to hold you accountable and hold them accountable. Be in service to them and they will be in service to you.

Have a rhythm that works for you. This rhythm doesn't have to be complicated, but something that will keep you connected to both your work and your personal life. Some days this might have to be adjusted, but if you start a daily routine and include all the important things in your life, you will start to see the integration changing your mindset. Your day won't just be work driven or just be family driven. When you create a rhythm that works for you, it becomes easier to manage your time, and easier to spend that time wisely.

Your life is precious and you have a purpose. Discover your weakness, and seek out failure because you will uncover your strength and learn through the process. Don't be afraid to fail or be vulnerable, but have faith that everything will mold and shift into the right places. Build a community of support and create a rhythm that works in your favor. It's important to leverage your time, so that you can focus on what is important in your life. When you find what is important to you in life, don't take it for granted.

Want to hear the full conversation, head on over to https://www.thebriancoveyshow.com/

Chapter 3

NADA LENA

Nada Lena has inspired me as a leader through her company, Rise Up For You, and the various places she has spoken for including TEDx and Google. Leadership became important to Nada after her first career, touring internationally as a singer and dancer. She came back to the United States and highlighted the top challenges that her team faced. In this chapter, I've gathered the tips and tricks Nada shared with me to master emotional intelligence and become a better leader.

NECESSARY SOFT SKILLS TO START DEVELOPING NOW

Having emotional intelligence is a primary soft skill that will make someone a better team member and a person in general. Developing emotional intelligence will create growth in a business and growth in each team member's life outside of the office. This one key factor will hit on every aspect of a person including confidence, self-management, and how they show up every day. Many sales teams have produced sales simply by enhancing an individual's confidence to talk on the phone or their ability to manage themselves while talking with a client that is not so kind. Those simple skills can be the game-changer for a lot of companies. On the leadership side of soft skills, there needs to be great communication, leadership, and the ability to include diverse team members. Emotional intelligence training is the key to starting the conversation of positive company culture with the people skills that are essential.

START WITH A POSITIVE COMPANY CULTURE

Many companies are spending a lot of time on cosmetic culture including big things like slides or even small things like bagels on Mondays. Those things are exciting, but at the end of the day they don't really transform people. There are two things in a company culture that are very important today:

- Psychological Safety: Being able to cultivate an environment and a culture where people can actually speak up in a positive way without fear of repercussions that are harmful to them.

- Growth Mindset: Having a culture of learning that is solution-driven. We should teach our team members that it is okay to voice your concern about something, but bring solutions or creative ideas. If there's no solution being brought up, then it just becomes complaining and then we can't solve anything.

These two things are the very first steps to having a positive company culture because your people are your product. People matter and cultures are made out of people. Here's a visual:

Culture> People> Product

So, if the culture is not good, then the people aren't going to be good, then the product is never going to be at its full potential, and then the clients are never going to get to experience the full potential of the company you have.

COLLECT DATA AND CONDUCT ANALYSIS

For success in any business, it is important to notice the employee turnover rate, and how often employees are engaged. If your business has a high employee turnover rate, then you need to take a step back and ask some hard questions. If your employees are just coming to work and doing their thing, but not really interacting, why is there a lack of engagement? One thing Nada suggested to do in this case, and at any stage of a business, is to do anonymous surveys.

It is helpful for businesses to have employees do anonymous surveys before they're in the company, while they're in the company, and most importantly when they exit the company because you want to understand first impressions, and why an employee might be leaving. Is it leadership? The culture? Are we not allowing them to grow? We need to do these surveys and analysis because it is possible to have a great product and bring in a ton of money, but not be able to sustain the success because you're not doing the work with your people.

When Nada was an executive, she had 200 staff members under her. She had an open-door policy and thought that she came off as approachable to her employees, even though she had a few people tell her that she is intimidating and hard to talk to. Finally, she did an anonymous survey with the entire 200 staff members because she wanted to be the best leader she could be. She encouraged everyone to be honest and say whatever they felt to be true because she wouldn't know who it was. About 75% of the staff members said that she was intimidating. With this feedback, she was able to see that she was not showing up as the person that she wanted to be.

BE AWARE, BE VULNERABLE, AND BE WILLING TO TAKE ACTION TO IMPROVE

After you go through the data and the team surveys, it's important to communicate the results and future actions with your business. If you find challenges after the data analysis and team surveys, then you need to address those challenges and actively work on them. If you are ignorant of the challenges of your business before you have feedback, that's one thing, but after you see proof of areas that you lack in as a leader, you have to take action to fix those areas. After Nada saw the results from her team surveys show that 75% of her employees found her to be intimidating, one of the first things she did was call it out.

She was transparent with her team. It was a vulnerable thing to do, but she spoke to all of her employees about how she was going to work on being less intimidating. As leaders, we don't want to come across as weak or vulnerable, but it's all about humanity. People appreciate it when a leader can take accountability and pick out the strengths and weaknesses of a business and actively start to work on them. People love that kind of transparency from a leader because now they are connected to you.

WHAT IS EQ?

Emotional intelligence, or EQ, is being able to identify, understand, and manage our emotions, as well as identify, recognize, and influence the emotions of others. There are two sides to the coin. There are four pillars that fall under EQ, that consist of the whole workforce and leadership.

THE FIRST TWO PILLARS HAVE TO DO WITH THE SELF...

1. Self-awareness: Being aware of your emotions and how you come across to others.

2. Self-management: How you manage your emotions, intrinsic motivation, and the ability to adapt.

THEN THE LAST TWO PILLARS HAVE TO DO WITH OTHERS...

3. Social awareness: Being able to have empathy, and understanding where people are coming from.

4. Relationship management: All things leadership. This includes team building, conflict resolution, influence, being able to coach people, and building relationships.

These four pillars are the construct of the entire workforce and the challenges that we see today with communication, diversity, inclusion, leadership, and empathy. It all falls under these four pillars. Then under the four pillars, there are 18 competencies that get even more in-depth such as motivation, accurate self-assessment, and self-confidence. These 18 competencies are the core of sustainable success for individuals and organizations.

HOW TO IMPROVE YOUR EMOTIONAL INTELLIGENCE

The most important concept behind EQ is accurate self-assessment. So, the first step is to figure out what you have to work on because we all have blind spots.

Making self-improvements means doing the work to find your strengths and weaknesses and how to improve on them. Nada explained that one of the best ways to do that is by taking a self-assessment, but that's the easy part. First, you take your assessment quiz and answer the questions honestly about how approachable you are, how confident you are, how good you are at communication, etc. Here's the tricky part, you'll give the same assessment quiz to about 5 to 10 people that you trust will give you honest feedback, and have them answer all of the questions in regards to you. Then you compare their honest assessment to your own assessment and seek out the areas that you need to improve.

Comparing your perception to others' perceptions will help you see if your assessment of yourself is accurate or if you have blind spots. Once you find those hidden weaknesses, you can take the necessary actions to improve them.

LEADERSHIP GUIDE

To be a good leader, you need to be a potential-seeker. Be a potential-seeker in yourself and in others. The more we can look at our team members and say "I know that there's more in there," and inspire them to be their best, the better the whole collective company is going to be. A lot of leaders miss that part of the process. They don't capitalize on the opportunities of looking at other individuals and helping them be their best. The fact is, a lot of individuals don't know how to do it until that leader pulls the potential out of them. Then they start to show up differently and produce differently. Cultivate the potential in yourself and constantly seek the potential in every one of your team members.

The thing about soft skills is that they are easy to comprehend, but they are difficult to take action on and implement. Unlike hard skills, which are difficult to comprehend. We might not be able to grasp the math, but once we get it, it's like autopilot. We learn that 2+2=4 and we don't forget it. With soft skills, you have to start by building the soft skill muscle, as an athlete would build muscle, so that you can be more productive, be a great leader, and have that career edge.

Want to hear the full conversation, head on over to https://www.thebriancoveyshow.com/

CHAPTER 4
MATT NEWMAN

M atthew Newman has been in the financial services industry since 1997, is a father to three small children, and was diagnosed with grade three astrocytoma (brain cancer) at 39 years old. His message is about living in the moment and appreciating the now, his story helps others gain clarity on what's really important in life, and his dedication to being a top performer at everything he does has led him to become number one in sales at his profession for over twenty years, while also fighting cancer. In this chapter, I've gathered the messages and inspiration from Matt for you to apply in your own life and business.

OVERCOME ADVERSITY AND LEVERAGE IT TO SERVE OTHERS

We learn some of the greatest lessons in life during the deepest darkest times. During those times, we can be gifted with a new set of lenses to see things in new ways. Our perspectives on our lives can change. It's often caused by a catastrophic event that we go through, but sometimes it can be too late. Sometimes we're no longer here physically to be able to take advantage of the new sense of reality that we can be gifted with.

Matt grew up just outside of New York City. His mother was a school teacher and his father was a financial advisor. He learned some great lessons early on that he used to become the successful businessman he is today. On the day that he graduated from college, his father asked him what he wanted to do, and his answer was to go work at his father's firm. Matt explained to me that his father taught him a valuable lesson that day and that is that there are no free lunches. You have to go out and earn what you want. You have to go out and find your craft, your calling, or something that you relate to and dive in headfirst.

His father gave him three pieces of advice before he went off on his own:

1. If you don't believe in the product or someone in your family won't own, don't sell it. It's about earning the respect and trust of consumers.

2. Always be honest. When you have honesty and belief, good things will happen.

3. Have a great work ethic. Use the work ethic that you used in sports or school and apply that to build your business.

As a brand new wholesaler in Philadelphia, Matt started his career using the skills that he already knew from his father. He knew that as a wholesaler, his job was to be there when things are bad and to give people good news. That's what financial planning provides, good news in deep and dark times

The education system doesn't teach anything about this. When most people hear the term "financial planning" they think it has to do with money. Financial planning actually has nothing to do with your money, and everything to do with your will, power of attorney, and life insurance. It's not how much money you have, it's that if you get incapacitated or something happens, your wishes will be carried out and your family will be protected. Many people are not educated on these things, but Matt was the opposite.

Matt knew these things and practiced what he preached. Then, in 2002 when the market crashed, his business shot up like a rocket and he became the #1 guy in the industry. His dad called him up and told him he would be willing to talk about him joining his firm now, but Matt's response was that his price was too high for him now. He found his calling and his own way of discussing planning. He had a different position and perspective for planning than the traditional financial advisor, and that was his advantage. His ability to easily gain new perspectives would serve him well down the road.

STRENGTH

One of the greatest lessons Matt discussed was the importance of being there for your loved ones. When Matt's father-in-law was diagnosed with pancreatic cancer, his wife was pregnant with their third child, and she would drive him 45-minutes back and forth to the University of Pennsylvania for chemo and radiation therapy. Matt described his wife's efforts as an inspiration to him and an honor to witness that kind of strength.

Strength gives you a new perspective. When Matt felt the strength that came from finding out he had brain cancer, there was no way he was letting go of it. If he was going to deal with that situation, there was no way he was going down without defining his legacy. He decided that cancer was just going to be along for the ride. He didn't want to be known as the cancer guy.

When Matt found out he had brain cancer, he described his thoughts as clicking into a fight mode. He never let himself think anything bad was going to happen. He never sat there and wallowed in the fear of it. Instead, he decided that if he was going down, he was going to fight all the way. You learn what strength by gaining new perspectives on situations.

Matt started to understand what it felt like to be living in the moment, being where his feet were. He understood how fragile things could actually be, and unfortunately, many of us don't learn these things until much too late. There are people that get diagnosed with certain diseases or have fatal accidents that never get to experience the joy of a new perspective. So, he took his gift that cancer gave him and used it to overcome his disease.

HAVE A POSITIVE MINDSET

If you have a good mindset, it doesn't matter what obstacles you face, you are winning. To see the wins of our lives, we have to step back and see the bigger picture. Matt was being a better dad, husband, and truly enjoying his life. He found that he shouldn't have had to go through such devastating events to get to his new outlook, but is glad that cancer gave him that gift.

ENJOY THE MOMENT

The biggest thing to take away from Matt's story of hope and inspiration is that you can make decisions before you have to. You have the power today to change your perspective and change the way you show up for your family or your business. Today, you have the power to realize how special life is and how important being in the moment can be. So, put down your phone for a moment, and enjoy the people and opportunities around you.

FINDING AN OUTLET

We all face times of adversity and one thing that you can do to decrease the negative impact is to find a catharsis for themselves, Matt's is writing. When Matt learned of his new obstacle, he started to write messages of optimism and positive perspective and send them out to friends and family. As optimistic as Matt was, he explained that you have to also find a place for fear, anger, and anxiety because as long as it can find a way out, it's not combustible. He found his outlet in writing, but he would never read a message again after he sent it out. That was his process of letting his emotions out. Four years into writing these messages, he had 20,000 people following my emails because I didn't have socials. People wanted real and raw messages, and Matt wasn't writing them for anyone but himself. So that was how Matt decided to write his book, Starting at the Finish Line, and it became a #1 seller on Amazon in four different categories.

MATT'S DIAGNOSIS

One day in 2013, Matt got into a car accident. He was heading up to do a meeting and his car starts to hydroplane, smashes right into the car in front of it, and flips over into the median. Matt had no injuries, but his wife reminded him of their friend, Karen. Karen had gotten into a car accident with seemingly no injuries but was told to go to the hospital to make sure she was okay. Two hours into her hospital visit, the doctors walk in and tell her to send flowers and a thank you note to the person that hit her because they found a brain aneurysm and she would've been dead three hours from then.

Even though the story his wife reminded him of was convincing, he decided to not go to the hospital. Then his head started to hurt, like a huge migraine. The pain got more severe over the next few weeks. Then one day while he's giving a speech, he started to feel like he was having a stroke. He shook it off and kept going. He started to have more and more of them, and he finally went to go get it checked out. They found that he had a lesion on the left frontal lobe of your brain that was causing him to have seizures, and he immediately assumed it was from the car accident weeks before. While the doctors were taking him to another MRI scan they said they needed to see how big his tumor was, and that was the moment he found out that he had brain cancer, at age 39.

MATT'S NEW MINDSET

Matt explained to me about how he felt when he first went home after getting the news, and how his kids greeted him with signs that said "I love you, daddy." He explained that that moment was his, he owned it, and he was going to start being there. That same week, his son had a bring your dad to lunch day. The goal of this event is to go eat brown bag lunches for 30-minutes with your kid. Matt mentioned that his wife told him that he didn't have to go to this because he looked like a mess, but he responded that he would never miss it in a million years. He went to lunch with a hat on and his 5-year-old son, Luke, spots him and runs to give him a big hug. They go sit at a picnic table and have lunch together. While he enjoyed lunch with his son, he noticed that every single dad there was glued to their phones. He had no anger or animosity because that was him before he started to see things differently. He knew that he had to go through the horrible storm he was in to learn that the 30-minute lunch wasn't about him, it was about his son.

He couldn't drive or do much of anything at a point, and his wife asked if he wanted to come to drop his 2-year-old daughter, Lola, off at school. He went and held his daughter's hand while they walked Lola to her class in her little pink coat, and she took her jacket and hung it on the little hook. Then she turned around and said, "Thank you, Daddy, I love you." He then thought about why he didn't do that more often. He replayed all the past times he might have done this and in all the scenarios he was on his blackberry or rushing off for work, but now that he had a newfound perspective on what was important, he made sure to stay in those precious moments for as long as he was able.

He realized that before he was diagnosed, he was teaching his children that it was okay to not acknowledge your family or have quality time together. He knew that he was winning whether cancer went away or not, he now had the mindset to see what was truly important to him. If you take nothing else from this chapter, **remember that your mindset can drastically change the outcome of any situation you encounter in your life.**

Want to hear the full conversation, head on over to https://www.thebriancoveyshow.com/

Chapter 5

Victor Maya

Victor Maya is a nationwide voice for culture building, positive thinking, and enabling minorities to structure their lives and businesses for success. After overcoming seemingly impossible challenges, he built a life based on his core values and now has over 10 years of experience building companies into million-dollar ventures.

As you read about Victor's life story, determination, and perseverance, reflect on your own motivators in your life and how you are setting yourself up for success every day.

The American Dream

At the young age of six, Victor and his family arrived in the United States from Pico De Paz, Mexico. The first things that he noticed when they arrived at I-45 were all of the tall, glass buildings in Houston, Texas. Victor remembered playing in the dirt and taking showers with a cup and a bucket and, at that moment, said to himself that he was going to do something amazing with this new opportunity. Once they got settled, his mother was always working two to three jobs, coming home at two in the morning, and doing everything possible to make sure her children were taken care of.

When he was 10 years old, he told his mother that he was going to fill a suitcase up with money in order to get her out of poverty, and he fulfilled that promise when he was 30 years old. However, it only took him that long because he was young, stuck, and selfish with the money that he earned. Victor saw his first million dollars when he was 22 years old, but since he was a kid with a large amount of money, he lost sight of the big dreams for his family that he had when he was 10. But nonetheless, he was able to keep his promise and conquer himself, his challenges, and poverty throughout the process.

Victor knew from a very young age that he wanted to create a life for himself, his family, and his future generations. He worked extremely hard over the years and had to maneuver his way through many challenges life threw his way. Not only was he growing, learning, and bettering his life, he was also making mistakes, failing, and having to come to tough realizations.

His childhood reminded him that when you have a lot in life, the little things and moments get pushed aside and you aren't able to see or be grateful for everything you have. However, when you have very little, the smaller moments and things seem so much bigger and more special. He remembers being amazed by the rocks in the creek that he played in as a child and how much joy they brought him at the time. But the more that he got in life, the harder it was to remember to see everything and be grateful for every small thing or moment. The more that you gain in life, always remember to take a step back and appreciate everything that you encounter and have. It doesn't matter how much money you have or how many things you have because you'll never be able to take anything with you.

BUILDING A STRONG CULTURE

One of Victor's passions is sharing his wisdom and knowledge that he has learned throughout his life with other people. Specifically, sharing and building with his team so that they are able to live a successful and positive life as well. You can have a perfect strategy plan, execution plan, and all of the money in the world but if you don't have a strong team and culture then you're not going to get far. He had to spend years building the culture that he has now and learned along the way that responsibility and accountability are crucial values in becoming a successful leader.

He was inspired to create a strong culture from a trip he took to the gas station one afternoon. At the station, there were tons of bikers that all drove Harley's. Victor noticed that there were white, brown, and black Harley's and there were tall people, short people, straight people, and gay people who were the owners because it didn't matter, as long as you drove a Harley you were considered to be a part of their family.

He wanted to create a work culture that represented that and began by establishing the team's core values and mission statement collectively. As a leader, it was also important to live as a representation for the rest of the team and take account-ability for the team's performance.

A friend of Victor's once told him, "Your values are not who you are right now, they are who you are going to be in the future" and he made sure to remember that he will always make mistakes but at the end of the day, he is growing into who he is meant to be.

NEVER BE AFRAID TO FAIL

Victor's message to his younger self and upcoming leaders is to always learn from your failure and to never fear failure. When his son was struggling with learning new information, he made him fail over and over again so that he could understand the benefits and success that comes from failing. Whenever you fail at anything in life, you have to ask yourself what you're going to do with the new information that you have learned from it and get back on track. The only possible way to truly lose or fail is to quit. People can take every last thing away from you, but they will never be able to take away what you know and your ability to get back up.

A common lesson that athletes are required to learn is to "do better once you know better", and this applies in everyday life. When a coach shows an athlete a mistake he made and how to fix it or begin working on fixing it, the athlete knows better than to operate the way he was before he learned the new information. Once you learn the lessons from failure, you have to execute what you have learned by physical action, and that is the hardest gap people have to cross every day. You have to take action. There is no power in knowledge without action.

Create Your System

At one point in his life, Victor was struggling with divorce, his health, and taking care of himself. A mentor of his pushed for him to get a health coach, write a book, and take hold of his life. Since English was not his first language and he had a hard time with grammar, the thought of writing a book himself seemed impossible. He knew that he is not the best writer, smartest or best person in his company but that is why he hires a team of people that can help with his weaker points and bring different strengths and gifts to the table. None of the best leaders have everything figured out and it's easy to fall into a trap of thinking that you have to be the best at everything and have it all figured out. Everyone has completely different strengths and weaknesses and that is why it is important to assemble a team of people that each help to fill different roles.

To work well on a team and make sure that everything runs smoothly, you should set systems in place to optimize overall wellbeing and teach your team to operate on the same system. Victor calls his system the "whole person" and breaks it down to mind, body, heart, and spirit.

IQ (Intellectual quotient), SQ (spiritual quotient), EQ (emotional quotient), and PQ (physical quotient) represent the four areas within a person that needs to be tended to every single day. Victor wakes up at four a.m. every morning and immediately tackles the spiritual component by journaling and praying to God. Afterward, he hits the intellectual component by reading and expanding his mind through different genres. His emotional quotient is met by spending quality time with his family, loving on people, and helping people. Finally, he fuels his body with proper nutrition and goes to the gym five times a week.

He emphasizes that when your balance scale tips and one or more of these areas isn't being met, your life will begin to trail off course. It doesn't matter if you make all of the money in the entire world and succeed in every business-related venture, at some point, it will crumble and be worth nothing. It will be forgotten about and won't live on. It is an honor to leave a legacy that your future generations can model their own lives after, that is why Victor views his journaling as a written legacy.

STRUCTURE YOUR DAY

In today's society, "I don't have enough time" is way too common of an excuse for not building habits or doing the things in life that you're passionate about. Victor truly believes that you do have time, it is just how you choose to manage your time that matters. He has created a system, a routine that he has done so many times that when he wakes up, he already knows that he is going to finish at two p.m. every day and it is ingrained as a habit in his unconscious mind. Also, he makes sure to get the hardest tasks done in the morning so that he is able to go about the rest of his day without neglecting or dreading the hardest tasks or conversations he needs to get done. All of his priorities are done between noon and two p.m. every single day and he is then able to coach his team and love on his people.

Victor wasn't always a system person. At one point he was treating ADD with 30 milligrams of Adderall a day, made excuses, played the victim, and was heavily unorganized. He then learned, through the help of others, how to create a system and reprogram his unconscious mind so that it became a habit that he didn't even have to talk himself into doing. Everyone struggles with not having enough time or not having a good enough mentality but focusing on the unconscious mind will help eliminate the excuses and create structure in your life that will benefit you heavily in the long run.

KNOW YOUR PRIVILEGE

If you were born in the U.S., you have to be aware of the privilege that you were already granted at birth. Victor is just one example of an immigrant with a dream for a better, happier future outside of poverty for him and his family, and there are millions of people who may not ever have the privilege of living in the United States. Not being born in the U.S. created hundreds of obstacles that he conquered for decades in order to live a comfortable life, which some people are already born into.

When he was 10 years old, Victor had to push a cart two miles from his apartment to the grocery store in order to pick up groceries they were paying for with food stamps. One day when his mother was using food stamps, a guy in the grocery line asked her how she was planning on paying society back after all that they had done for them. At the time, they were receiving food stamps and Medicaid. Given that his mother didn't speak English, Victor had to translate the conversation to each of them, and he responded to the man by saying that his mother will never be able to pay society back. But someday, he would be able to pay society back in ways that the man could not imagine. From there, he started moving forward. He knew that he was going to overcome all of these challenges, no matter the circumstances, in order to pay society back, help his family, and live a more stable life.

He did something that could easily be viewed as impossible while also bettering himself, his family, and his team along the way. Victor truly conquered every obstacle in his life, and by doing so, is now able to add value and meaning to so many others.

Want to hear the full conversation, head on over to https://www.thebriancoveyshow.com/

Chapter 6
EVAN STEWART

This chapter covers the words of Evan Stewart, a world-renowned life, business strategist and founder of Obsessed Academy. He is most commonly sought-after regarding clarity, purpose, calling, obsession, and expertise in scaling companies and driving profits for different levels of organizations. Evan combines individual purpose with business to help others build and achieve a life that they can be obsessed with.

You don't get to where you are meant to be by chance, read on to learn how you can build towards where you're going in life.

FINDING YOUR PURPOSE

You have most likely heard the common phrase, "love what you do." This is normally used when describing career choices in an effort to have someone choose a path that they love and find their purpose. Evan believes that you shouldn't do what you love, but rather, you love aspects of what you do. We have to realize that our business was built to serve our life, not our life for our business, so there are aspects in our daily work that can pull out the gifts that are inside of us.

Love is simply just a chemical reaction most of the time, not a consistent and sustainable emotion. You can easily fall in love with something because you are in the honeymoon phase of something brand new, but that doesn't mean that it is going to last. The excitement that someone feels during their very first soccer game isn't going to remain constant, and the actor that gets his first feature won't feel that same exact rush on his 20th job. There is an ambiguous definition around love that is different for each and every person, therefore it's not sustainable. Sustainability always needs to be applied, regardless of how you feel.

The key to finding your purpose is to challenge yourself to realize what comes naturally to you that is difficult for other people. Often, our gifts and our purpose are wrapped in packaging that we overlook because it comes naturally to us and we don't have to apply a lot of effort to it.

We all have something independently that comes extremely naturally to us and we don't have to apply the same effort towards it that others do. For example, Evan doesn't think in terms of math and it does not come easily to him, however, his brother has a very analytical mind and is brilliant at math because it is naturally how his brain operates.

He swears by a three-step process to help figure out where you are meant to add value and how you can build an impact.

1. Awareness

2. Intention

3. Engagement

First is becoming aware of what you can do that comes naturally and doesn't come as freely to other people. An easier way to figure this out is to ask yourself "What do people come to me for that has nothing to do with my job profession." For instance, Evan found that many people called on him when they had hard challenges going on in their lives and needed someone to talk to.

Next, moving with intention or developing discipline and obedience to work the muscle of awareness. Now, when someone calls Evan and says that they are struggling, he intentionally builds the conversation in a way that he can reflect on it, pull value from it, and do it consistently.

Finally, the engagement piece says that you are going to, with purpose, dive deep, and intentionally engage with this gift. Instead of waiting for a phone call, Evan now picks up the phone and reaches out to his friend first to see how they are doing and to let them know that they were in his heart. He purposefully goes out of his way to work that muscle.

Evan personally defines purpose as "The thing in your life played through the thing in your life that you do that doesn't come naturally to other people and in that work, it positively and meaningfully impacts the life of another individual and has the potential to positively shift the life of other people in your life that you touch through it forever."

The purpose is of such heavy significance that we have to give it that weight so that it demands the attention it deserves to actually create the impact.

LEADING WITH PASSION AND PURPOSE

If you are in a professional environment, a leader's job is to ensure that the vision an employee or team member has for their life can be encompassed by the mission you have as an organization. Evan believes that you need to be inspired, fascinated, and motivated by where you live, work, who you live and work with, and how you live and work. Inspiration is what gets you going, fascination is the thing you can get positively lost in, and motivation is the thing that keeps you going. When you wake up and that drive is not there, motivation fills in that role and pushes you to keep going despite not entirely feeling like doing so.

As a leader, it is your job to make sure that your work environment encompasses these key qualifiers because part of a leader's responsibility is to help their team wake up ignited and go home fulfilled. Human beings work better, have better teams, are more supported, function better, and have happier clients if someone is actually excited to walk in the door because they know they are going to be appreciated, seen, heard, acknowledged, and fulfilled when they leave.

Having your own purpose figured out as a leader helps you to better coach your team on the steps to discover their own and make sure the company's mission builds on these values.

COMBATING DISTRACTIONS WITH DISCIPLINE

Quarantine specifically has highlighted the huge roadblock of daily distractions from our goals, but it has always been a problem. From social media to constant texts and phone calls from clients and loved ones, it can be extremely hard to silence the outside world and stay dedicated to what we are currently working on.

One of the best ways that Evan recommends preventing distractions from interfering is to never justify or apologize for the way that you choose to work. We often get physically distracted, but the root of it is actually because we haven't created an environment for ourselves where we can say "this is not the time for us to speak, we are going to have to talk later," and the other person is not offended or hurt. Therefore, the distraction exists because the environment allows it to.

He also operates by the one-touch-rule, which means that if he is currently working on it there will not be anything other than an emergency that will pull his hands off of it until he is done.

These two things have created an airtight environment for Evan and have allowed his productivity to improve significantly. He can put his phone on Do Not Disturb and everyone understands that it is not a personal matter, but rather he needs the space and time to accomplish what he needs to get done for the day.

GET OBSESSED WITH YOU

You have to go all-in and be obsessed with what you do or else it is most likely not worth doing. This knowledge pushed Evan to create the Obsessed Academy, a program that provides education, training, and resources to grow companies through increasing revenue, vested relationships, and establishing strong foundations.

In order to build a life that you are obsessed with, you have to be consistent. Evan's first suggestion is to always touch discomfort every single day whether that's waking up early, working out in the morning, or even if it's just forcing yourself to get up early and being lazy. You have to reach a small level of discomfort to build the muscle.

Not all obsession is negative and Evan believes that healthy obsession is necessary and a driving force to living your best life. A healthy obsession can be broken down into a three-part cycle.

Its emotion, a moment of revelation, and feeling.

Second, obsession is a mindset and a season of preparation. You cannot prosper where you are planted unless you first take root in where you are placed. We are often called before we are competent, and we think that we are supposed to be harvesting when in reality we are supposed to be planting.

Third, it is a discipline that is a moment of cultivation. Cultivation stirs up the motivation because as you see more and more in your harvest, you strive for more and begin to plan for the upcoming seasons and years

Evan compares a healthy obsession with a fruit tree. The first harvest of a fruit tree is extremely weak, and with every bloom, it gets fuller until years down the road it finally blossoms into a full-grown, healthy tree. But it cannot become a full, blossomed fruit tree until it goes through multiple different seasons and harvests.

Having grace, space, and patience in regard to where you are at is key. Evan no longer has anxiety that his life isn't getting better because he knows he is not supposed to be reaping his rewards yet, he is meant to be planting seeds. Oftentimes the issue is that individuals don't realize that they are in a healthy obsession cycle because they had a vision or a feeling that they were supposed to be five steps ahead, but they haven't yet walked.

If you start to feel the anxiety about being farther along, ask yourself if you are still in a season of preparation and look at where your roots are actually growing before complaining that you are not reaping yet.

EVANS BACKGROUND

Evan grew up in a family of entrepreneurs and was constantly taught about problem-solving and recognizing a need. One summer at his great uncle's lake house, he was being asked about school and how it was going for him and his friends. Instead of asking about homework or recess, he would ask him "What problems are you encountering," and by doing so he was creating a paradigm shift. He'd then ask how many of his friends are having the same problem and if those people would ever want his help solving the problem. Although these issues as a child actually didn't matter, it started wiring Evan's brain to begin thinking like an entrepreneur and where to look for opportunities. To this day he has only worked retail for three months of his life and helped his father out for summer, other than that, he has never worked for someone else and has always created his own opportunities.

He used this exact same framework and developed Obsessed Academy out of recognizing a need and seeing how it fit into his life. About five years into his real-estate company that he built basically from the ground up, he became aware that people were calling him with questions about their own lives and careers. He continued to answer all of the questions that he got and noticed that more and more people were calling with similar questions. One day someone asked him if he had ever considered coaching and he answered with, "Sure, why not? A thousand bucks." She replied, "Sounds great, I'm in."

More and more clients began scheduling coaching with him throughout the next weeks, and all of a sudden, he is building a multi eight-figure business and found himself starting to utilize his purpose and his gifts that came easily to him. He poured more energy into those areas and soon sold his company and built the Obsessed Academy. In his own life, Evan displayed awareness, intention, and engagement to develop his passion and purpose.

Want to hear the full conversation, head on over to https://www.thebriancoveyshow.com/

CHAPTER 7
DAVID MELTZER

David Meltzer is a speaker, entrepreneur, author, and co-founder of Sports 1 Marketing. He began his journey teaching people how to make money but has since changed his goal to empowering people to be happy, 1 billion to be exact. Throughout his life, David encountered many learning experiences that he believes will help and inspire others.

Speaking with him challenged me to take a look at my own life and what I have chosen to prioritize. This chapter will open up your eyes to the true values and meaning of life while also showing you how he went from "not enough" to "just enough."

VALUES ARE THE KEY

David spent the early years of his life striving towards monetary and external gain. When he reached the age of 30, everything that he valued took a huge shift. He realized that money was not the entryway to happiness and that there was much more in life that is far more valuable. He lost who he was and what he truly valued in the pursuit of success but learned that who you are as a person, what you chose to value and the value that you give to others in life is the true key to happiness.

It is important to take inventory of your values every single day and not be afraid to change your values as you are growing. It's okay to say, "What I believed to be valuable yesterday is not what I find valuable today." He has found that there are four main values to living a happy, influential life.

1. <u>The first key to living a happy life is to have the perception of gratitude.</u> That means no matter what's happening externally to you, that you have the capability of finding light, love, and lessons in everything.

He used to view pain differently but now sees it as a mental, physical, spiritual, emotional, and financial indicator that he has to learn to go in a better direction or make something or a situation better. Life lessons will keep coming until you learn them and will result in pain when you haven't learned them.

2. <u>The second value is forgiveness.</u> When you're expanding and growing, you're going to make a ton of mistakes. If you make a ton of mistakes, you are going to have to learn to forgive yourself. If you can't forgive yourself, you're going to live in ego-based consciousness, meaning you're going to create resistance between you and the greatest source of light, love, and lessons that exists. You're also going to create resistance, void shortages, obstacles, interference with everyone else in the world, and everything else that is connected to forgiveness as a means.

Forgiveness is a means to unwind or clear all of the interference or corrosion to not only that great source of power, love life lessons, but everything else. All those other relationships and ventures and opportunities that you have. Everything you're connected to.

3. <u>The third is accountability.</u> Accountability gives you control. This is extremely important right now because so many people feel that they are out of control. There are so many variances in life right now, so many instabilities, so much inundated information about the variances and the instabilities, and the compressed uncertainty. Being in control of yourself just takes only one thing, accountability.

David believes that this means to ask yourself two questions, "What did I do to attract this into my life?" and "What am I supposed to learn from it?" No blame, no shame, and no justification. It was attracted into your life and it is your job to figure out what you are supposed to learn from it without placing blame or being overrun with guilt. If you combine forgiveness and gratitude you get the fourth value, inspiration.

4. <u>Inspiration is different from motivation because motivation is only temporary and drives you with energy until it doesn't last anymore.</u> It will help get you back up and help get you started, but it won't get you there. Inspiration gets you there by living with this connection, allowing it to come through you, and knowing the more you receive from the light, the love, and the lessons the more you learn. The more you can give to others this idea of the abundance of the world.

Gratitude, forgiveness, accountability, and inspiration are the four key mechanisms to get you through rough periods of life.

3 Types of Listeners

In all ages, industries, and professions, people aren't interested. They're just interesting. They've lost the fine art of listening. David describes three types of listeners, there's the interrupter, the waiter, and there is someone who is more interested than interesting. The waiter never actually listens to what you say, they are only waiting to tell you what they want to say.

But the person who is more interested than interesting is processing what you are saying, learning from you, and trying to enhance more knowledge, skills, and capabilities from you to elevate others. In life, it's easy to fall into being an interrupter or a waiter, but it is extremely important to become more interested than interesting in conversations.

Overcome Ego-Based Consciousness

The ego is a complex term containing multiple different interpretations, but David speaks of the ego as a limiting, self-centered way of thinking.

Forgiveness is one of his core values to living a happy life, and yet it is one of the hardest to achieve. It is extremely hard for people to be able to forgive themselves because we are our own worst critics, and our ego takes control. The ego will easily edge goodness and happiness out of your life if you let it. It says things like "I can't be responsible for this, I can't forgive myself, I'm not worthy, I'm inferior, I'm superior, I'm angry, worried, anxious, frustrated, I'm guilty." We all have these ego-based corrosive experiences, instead of saying the truth which is, "I'm human, I'm connected to everything and everyone." And the only way that you can expand, accelerate, and appreciate positivity and happiness is to make mistakes.

The only way to get past the mistakes of learning is to forgive yourself because you don't know what you don't know.

You are learning and growing every single day and there is no benefit to punishing yourself for not knowing what you didn't know yesterday.

MONEY IS NOT THE KEY TO HAPPINESS

David was born into a world of not enough. His mother was a single mom who worked tirelessly to make ends meet for her family and he connected the dots at a very young age that if they had more money, the stress would be alleviated, and they would have no boundaries in the way of reaching happiness. Only nine months out of law school, David made his first million dollars. Everything from that point on reaffirmed that money bought happiness and he became a multi-millionaire CEO of the world's most notorious sports agency, Leigh Steinburg Sports and Entertainment.

At age 30, David received a birthday gift from his father who left when he was five years old. It was a nice sport coat that, when he put it on, had the pockets removed. He immediately became enraged and called his father to understand why he had ruined his birthday gift on purpose. His father told him it was to remind him that money cannot buy happiness. "You're just like me. I don't want you to be the richest man in the cemetery. I want you to hang the jacket in the closet to remind you that money doesn't buy happiness and that you can't take anything with you when you're gone. Don't make the same mistakes that I made at 30." Given that David's life was centered around money buying happiness, he became distraught and angry.

After that, his best friend told him that he didn't like who he had become and who he chose to surround himself with and his marriage was on the brink of divorce. His life felt completely empty and he was ready to call his lawyers when he looked in his closet and saw the jacket hanging. Still to this day, David gets choked up when sharing his story. His entire life shattered in front of him and he realized that his father was right, he hated his father because he hated himself. From then on, he began to take inventory of his values and shifted his life into living in abundance. Money is not the key to happiness and never was. Your happiness lies in your values and the value that you share with others.

Everything is a Setup, Not a Setback

David's philosophy is that you start with your angle with where you want to be and if you end up somewhere better, then you end up somewhere better. Every single thing in life is a setup, not a setback, and it is important to remember this when your life takes a turn that you hadn't planned on taking. You might have stumbled, fallen, and gotten bruised along the way but you pick yourself up and learn to be happy through the good times and the bad because you are constantly learning and growing.

It's easy to get caught up in the stress, chaos, and challenges that are thrown your way in life. Guilt quickly interrupts your happiness and keeps you from growing into the person you are meant to be. Don't take life so seriously. You don't know what you don't know, and every mistake that you make is teaching you new lessons.

Ferocious Buddha

One Saturday morning, David woke up to find his 17-year old daughter's car missing from their house at 4 a.m. Almost instantly, he went into a rage and almost called her freaking out and demanding to know where she was at. Right before he was finished dialing her number is when he identified that he had entered ego-based consciousness. Because he is a ferocious buddha, he paused, took a deep breath, and asked himself why he was so angry. Quickly he realized that he was just scared for his daughter's safety because he loves her so much and brought himself back to center. He called his daughter and learned that she was safely inside and had left her car at a grocery store because she was advised to never drink and drive. Since David decided to calmly approach the situation without anger, he preserved his and his daughter's relationship. Had he approached it yelling, he would have shamefully learned that she was safe and actually made the wise decision not to bring her car home. Taking a moment when life throws you off balance to stop and think about how you are truly feeling can save you from a lot of damage.

However, we are all still human and will have to deal with feeling unhappy, stressful emotions. David is even actively learning how to bring himself back to center and not let his emotions get in the way of his rational thinking. But, things in life that might normally ruin someone's day or cause them to lash out only brings him off-center for a few moments. He is capable of this because he practices ending fear, which is normally disguised as anger. People who have no control, no practice of ending fear, accelerate in the wrong direction so far. You need to practice ending fear and you will get to achieve and manifest everything you desire rapidly and accurately, especially happiness.

Want to hear the full conversation, head on over to https://www.thebriancoveyshow.com/

Chapter 8

Anthony Trucks

Anthony Trucks has been an American Football player since he was a young boy. He has overcome many life struggles throughout his journey. After realizing the NFL was not his calling, he became a transitional life coach. His goal as a speaker is to give advice on how using your identity can help you achieve your dreams if you understand it and utilize it. His message revolves around self-healing and finding your individual identity and using it to shape your mindset. In this chapter, I've collected the various messages and lessons from Anthony for you to apply throughout your daily life.

Life has a funny way of dealing us a set of weird, intimating cards, to say the least.

We learn some of the hardest lessons early on in life, especially when you're least expecting it. Finding yourself throughout these challenges is the goal for anyone planning on healing from certain childhood trauma. Anthony Trucks grew up a foster kid and did not find his current family until the age of six. His life was completely transitional and sudden, which instilled a great deal of strength within him. If anyone knows anything about overcoming obstacles at a young age, it's Anthony.

Mindset is a tricky subject because not many of us know how to tap into the inner working of our brain. Anthony became a speaker and a best-selling author after leaving the NFL, proving how unexpected shifts will happen throughout your life. Shifts are the catalysts for becoming the person you were truly meant to be

Anthony discussed ways to take these weird cards life gives us, and turn them into ways in which you can solidify your identity.

YOU CAN HAVE BOTH A GREAT MINDSET AND IDENTITY

If you do not self categorize with your mindset, it is ultimately useless. Anthony explained how much he sucked at his business career, yet had a great mindset. This example is just scratching the surface of how powerful your mindset can be. Our world today can be wrapped up in a false reality of the world, insisting they need to grow off of the vine of another individual. The identity you blossom into has to be fully crafted from your own hands.

Anthony found that studies have shown that if you do not categorize with your mindset, the mindset is almost of no use. Essentially what happens is this mindset becomes just like a piece of fruit. Once the fruit falls off the tree, then the fruit dies. After losing something that was once ours triggers the "Oh this sucks."

IT'S DIFFERENT TO SAY "I'M BOXING" OR "I'M A BOXER

One of the biggest lessons Anthony discusses was that the key to finding a great mindset is to shift from not just trying to be that thing, but becoming the full person. Mindset begins when self-realization is practiced and self-love is present.

We all have had our world pre-programmed for us throughout our life. He explains how a lot of people are waking up in 2020 with this hardware of a body. But they're running software like Windows 95. No one has made an upgrade to the human body in a real-world sense. Because we still operate how we used to 20 years ago? It is getting harder to operate life on your terms.

FLOW DETERMINES YOUR PERFORMANCE, YOUR PERFORMANCE DETERMINES YOUR SUCCESS

Anthony explained how identity is in fact who you are when you are not thinking about who you are. It is everything between your resiliency and your discipline, all the way to consistency. Once the identity train begins, it will only bring you to new realizations. Living your day to day life with content and positive energy will flow into your performance in your career field or relationships with people.

Before you flourish in your career field, it is important to discover that self-identity and become comfortable with it. Think of it this way, to find your flow, you have to identify as the successful, radiant person you want to be. This is an entire process within itself, but it will fuel the fire toward executing the performance you desire.

Now that you are self-aware, visualize the goals, meditate on them for a little bit. Think of ways to get yourself out of the little bubble of opportunities you see executable for society. Embrace who you are because the most successful people did not follow the status quo. Writers have to reinvent new ways of describing a feeling over and over again, so we have to be unique. Odds are, you aren't as bad as you think you are. Be you, no one else has your ideas.

WHAT YOU CREATE, CREATES YOU

Upgrades and successes in your life do not come easily. But, there is beauty in creating a version of yourself that you will want to invest in overtime. The longer you invest in yourself amidst a painful situation, the easier it will be to get yourself back up if life knocks you down. Strong people were crafted through years and years of pain and misfortunes, and they always get back up.

Anthony explains how the creative process is long and arduous and nobody goes through that whiteout receiving something in return. Yes, if you put good into the universe, it will give it back to you. And if you're thinking, "There's no way I can become a New York Times Best-Selling author," think about the daily steps you are taking to achieve that goal. Are you fighting for it? Are you putting every ounce of your passion into it?

You have the right to fight for what you deserve. Anthony reminisced on his early football years and explained how good he became after a full year of physical training. And then suddenly next year, he's the man. He became what he created, and everyone can do the same.

To reach your full potential, get rid of the idea that you do not deserve your dreams. People are not creating because they do not see the beautiful potential in every one of their goals. He discussed how feeling the pain and stepping up to the plate when life hands you cards is the best way to heal from them. Visualize your potential and learn from your mistakes, the best version of your identity will shine through.

SHIFT METHOD

One of the main things Anthony discusses in his speeches is how often people are not taught how to create actions to fulfill their goals. He created a plan called the Shift Method which uncovers the three ways we can discover our full potential.

See: Visualize and decide what you want to dive into. What is something you have been wanting to do all your life? And just decide you are going to do it. Also, remember to think about ways you can create a better identity within these goals.

Shift: This is when you grow. Shift into the reality you wish to see and start putting in the work. Involve other people because success doesn't begin alone. Listen to advice and ask the hard questions that ponder your mind.

Sustain: Strip down that ego that's protecting the bad part of your identity. Sustain the parts that are leftover. Appreciate who you are, and just do the work.

The world has been put under very unexpected circumstances this year and shifts were taking place in everyone's lives. Anthony's life was meant for rising to challenges, especially during his time in the NFL, but if you have a dream, understand that demand will come along with it. Stay true to who you want to be. He explains how he thinks of himself as a tree, and since he knows how to navigate his identity he is grounded. Trees around him are leaning back and forth, almost coming out of the ground. What sets him apart?

If you are trying to achieve something, remember it is normal to fail a couple of times. Keep yourself grounded by realizing the mistake, do what you can to change it, and lean back in. Step back up. He explains that once you start learning from the ups and downs of a situation, the better you will be at performing at a high level.

People sometimes do not want to hear the truth when it comes to discovering their identity. But when life hands you that weird deck of cards, know how to react to it. Anthony explained how in difficult times over the years, he has asked himself a very important question:

ASK YOURSELF: "WHAT DOES THIS MOMENT NEED FOR MY REALITY?"

Anthony has crafted who he is as a person after years of experience, and he has a list of things that must go into his week every week. Certain things in his morning routines keep him motivated and eager to work on new projects. Carving out time for your new projects is important, as long as you're working around your life. Keep your priorities number one but set time aside to work on what you truly want to work on.

Self-love and healing should always be at the top of your to-do list. Building upon what breaks, drives, or renews you is what changes perspective, and like the seasons change your landscape. Anthony is living proof that you can struggle with your identity and still come out on the other side with the identity that you've always dreamed of.

Want to hear the full conversation, head on over to https://www.thebriancoveyshow.com/

CHAPTER 9
RICH REDMOND

Rich Redmond is a creative superhuman and has been touring with musicians like Jason Aldean for the past two decades. While obtaining 26 number one hits and becoming an author and entrepreneur, Redmond is the perfect example of what it is like to learn from the different seasons we experience in life. Since the outbreak of coronavirus in March 2020, Redmond has continued to do live concerts via zoom and believes that our world will forever have a lasting impact from the tumultuous year we have all had.

Society has had to learn how to adapt to new human social behaviors because unfortunately, Redmond has also been studying acting for five and a half years and taking online classes to expand his knowledge. He truly is all about expanding his creative craft and refining the qualities that are going to make a positive impact on the world. In his classes, Redmond sees the waiters and baristas of our society and understands how scary it is to throw yourself into the deep end during this pandemic.

Staying positive and doing little things for yourself, yes that even been hydrating five times a days "That's why it's more important than ever to, to try to stay grounded with either like self-reflection, meditation growth, watching great films, eating great food, and making time for yourself," said Redmond. The hustle and bustle of life are great, but if you don't take care of yourself, it's only doing more damage than good. There is no way that your mental and physical connection can remain balanced if you are constantly running in circles. Change where you put your frame, start putting it in the mirror you are facing.

COMMIT TO YOUR PASSIONS, BUT EXPECT THE WORK TO COMMIT YOU

Redmond used to read positive literature which is where he tends to get his words of wisdom from. He gained a solid work ethic by doing labor like shoveling snow and waiting tables, which is where he gets his drive for commitment. When he discovered his true passion, he took pen to paper and wrote down all of his goals.

It gets real when you write it down. Redmond told himself that he was going to be a top recording drummer based in Nashville. He laminated this goal and put it everywhere around him. Most people expect their dreams to come to within a certain set of months or days, but the odds of that happening is slim. The things that you want to become reality may take up to five years in Redmond's case. Keep revisiting what you wrote down, the words won't come alive on their own.

BE POLITELY CONSISTENT

Not everyone in this world can be the best selling artist or be a professional soccer player. Why? Because being the best at your craft takes consistency. That little percentage of the people who can crack through the door and have the tenacity and the thick skin are the people who will get to where they want to be.

You have to fall in love with rejection because the more times you fall, the easier it is to get back up. Successful people have the vision to cultivate a career whether it's professional sports or the music business, it is like the Wild West, there are no rules. The only thing that's going to save you is your persistence.

There are always going to be sacrifices that you are going to have to make when trying to grasp your goals. When your friends want to go party, you may have to hit the books for a couple of hours or practice aligning your fingers with the right chords. The little sacrifices you make every day will be worth it in the long run because you love it And if you love what you do, it makes it easier to work hard because it doesn't even feel like hard work. Love what you do, and do what you love, that rush of golden happiness will follow.

Redmond talked about how fortunate he felt to know what his passion was from such a young age. "I feel like it was almost a gift from God and the heavens above that in 1976 I discovered my talent and I chased it. By the time MTV was born in 1981, and the Police's records came out in 1983, I had already found my purpose between 11 and 13 years old. I told myself I was going to for this, and here we are all these years later," said Redmond. He is 50 years old now and believes that politely pursuing your dreams, whether it takes decades or not, is the only way to be not only the most evolved human but to earn the spot you deserve.

SOMETIMES YOU HAVE TO TAKE A STEP BACK, TO TAKE A STEP FORWARD

When Redmond was starting his drumming career, he learned that to become successful as a musician, you needed to be in a big city. While he was playing on McDonald's jingles, he realized that he needed to get some outside help to get to the next level which was recording. Someone he knew said people like Trisha Yearwood and Dina Carter were auditioning for these spots, so he took matters into his own hands and stepped out of the shadows.

He was given positive feedback from people that were auditioning him, but he found that the one issue was that he did not live in Nashville. Immediately he knew that he had to step back in order to advance in his career. This is also where sacrifice comes into play we discussed early. There was no way the process was going to be smooth sailing, but he knew it was going to put exactly what he needed to get into the right doors.

As an entrepreneur or artist, you are constantly being told to "be your best self" or "just do what needs to be done for your benefit" and in this case, that is true. You have to be the best you because you are the salesman for your product, you.

Redmond talked about how he had to have good interpersonal skills and a firm handshake when looking people in the eye. He remembered names and uniquely displayed himself via eye contact and good conversation. Odds are, if the important people do not remember you then they are not going to reach out and contact you again. You have to convince people to buy into you because your brand is you.

You Have To Get Out And Let People Know You Exist

Social media is a huge tool in how creatives express themselves, especially musicians. Redmond tells us how he was using MySpace instantly and was trying to make international relations so people outside of his basement knew he existed and that he was different.

No one is going to be on board with something they have never seen before, because people do not like change or aesthetics that are out of the blue. People in society have certain ideas of how people in the entertainment industry should be, and it tends to be in a tiny glass box.

Redmond was an early adopter of social media and believes that this is a free tool to let the world know that you exist and what your message is. He said, "There is nothing more effective than using Instagram and other outlets to promote your vibe." The essence you want to spread will linger off of your social media and into other people's minds. And they will keep coming back. It will cut a lot of the excess noise out of your creative career.

FIVE PILLARS TO SUCCESS:

Redmond talked about his five main takeaways from his experiences that have made him the well rounded and successful person he is today. Use these in your everyday meditation or thoughts, write them down, and persist.

Commitment: The first step to becoming successful is to make a commitment to yourself in your mind, and start putting in the hours towards your craft. If you cannot set the goal straight in your head, then the odds of it becoming reality are incredibly slim. Doors are going to be slammed in your face, but this is normal.

Relationships: Cultivating mutually beneficial lifelong relationships by learning from your mistakes and becoming comfortable within yourself. Your reputation will precede you, so be careful about what you may say to your peers or bosses.

Attitude: This is the one thing everyone will remember about you, it's contagious. Even on your worst days, try and put a smile on your face and move forward.

Skill: Develop the skills you need to be successful in your chosen field, but never rest on your laurels. Because the world is moving so fast and we have to run just a standstill. It's important to continue developing new skill sets.

Hunger: No matter what season of your life you are in, you want to stay hungry for success. Stay tapped into that mindset you had when you were a little kid playing the drums, embrace the passion, and remember why you started working in the first place.

EVOLVE, BUT DON'T LOSE THAT CHILDLIKE FIRE

Artists have to be reinventing themselves for them to remain relevant. You have to grow and grow and then grow some more. You're essentially routing on the vine. Redmond discussed how at the end of the day, all he wants to do is affect people in positive ways and change lives. He did this through education, entertainment, and with her words to paper. The drummer inside of him did not want to let go of his dreams, so he didn't.

Diversifying the way you achieve your goals may spark new ideas or new connections. Double down and be methodical about developing new skills in your career. Redmond continues his education and even teaches because of his desire to be a positive light. "Learning new ways to breathe new sparks into your creative space is the same thing that I've been doing since 1976," said Redmond.

The people around Redmond have been an amazing resource for him and it all comes from him deciding not to be shy. He rose to every occasion and evolved, but did not lose that childlike fire. Out of all of the pillars of success, hunger is the most important piece because what drives hunger is your desire, and your desires are what continue to light the fire in you.

Want to hear the full conversation, head on over to https://www.thebriancoveyshow.com/

CHAPTER 10
BRIAN COVEY

As I mentioned at the beginning of the book, there's a possibility of my own tips and strategies finding their way into a chapter. Well, here it is. Here we will go over social media's role in business, what the modern leader looks like, and tactics to help you develop a strong team. These are all topics I've had experience with through being the Vice President of a home mortgage company and playing professional soccer.

My main focuses throughout my personal and professional life are to be constantly learning and growing. These are some of my personal tips and strategies I've picked up along the way...

THE VALUE OF SOCIAL MEDIA IN BUSINESS

Many industries, specifically mortgages that I'm in, have ignored the value of social media in business for too long. Other industries have capitalized on it way faster than us. Traditional mortgage companies or local mortgage professionals are either on there to stalk around or to try to figure out how to leverage it. About three years ago, I started to recognize shifts happening in my own business. People started going on their phones more, being on Facebook, and connecting through social media. A few people started to connect with me on social media, so I realized that I should start to do the same. If these people were reaching out to me, and I was willing to connect with them then there are probably other people that might want to do business with me if I reached out to them in the right way, by connecting with them. Not trying to send them my pitch to sell them, but by actually connecting with them. There is something about social media that reaches a wider audience than just making phone calls does. The skill of doing business through social media was not gained overnight. As I said, it took me three years to gain 60,000+ followers on Instagram and 32,000+ followers on LinkedIn. I had to work at it and learn a different way of business.

"You're never too old to dream a new dream." - C. S. Lewis

This quote resonated with my situation because I came into the social media game late, but I saw that this was a big trend in business. Instead of shying away because I was "too old for that" I learned how to do it and it helped my business grow. I mentioned all the followers that I gained, but it was not about followers. It's about making human connections

Social media business strategies are not about followers. They never were, and many professionals are beginning to realize that because you could have 50K followers or 100 followers, but your business only grows if those followers engage with your business. The goal is to have all 100 of your followers be real fans of your business. So, if you've gained 50K followers and only 100 of them are really fans you've missed the point and done more work in the wrong places. The biggest secret to doing business on social media is to build actual connections with your followers. That's how you create real clients and supporters who will refer and connect you to other clients or professionals in your field.

BUILD REAL CONNECTIONS ON SOCIAL MEDIA

One simple way that I build connections with my followers is to comment on their posts. Always respectfully, of course, and never anything critical about how they should change their lighting or camera set up. I comment something encouraging to boost them up because that is what we all fear most on social media… what if people don't like my content? My message? My style? We all want to feel validated and what better way to build a connection than through boosting someone's confidence on their social media posts? This action invites that follower to be engaged on your social media posts as well. One simple comment like "great post," "amazing story," or "this message is powerful" can be the starting point to a true connection. If nothing else, it increases the chances of that follower taking a second look at your profile to see who you are and what you do. That means that whenever they need a service you provide, they will think back to you and be more comfortable contacting you for business.

NETWORKING ON SOCIAL MEDIA

As a business leader, I've found that social media can connect you to many opportunities for new clients, new employees, and new professionals in your field. The goal of a business account is to seek out new clients and retain existing ones, and one way to do that is through networking with other professionals in your field. For example, if you are a real estate agent on social media and you come across another real estate agent account that has a similar brand to yours and a different area, it's a good opportunity to build a connection with them.

CLOSED CAPTIONING

Videos on social media is a huge trend. People enjoy watching videos rather than just seeing a million pictures. One fundamental tactic I have found to draw in followers is closed-captioning. People aren't always able to turn on their volume for various reasons. So when someone scrolls to your video and there are no closed-captions, they scroll past it because they can't listen to it at that moment. If there are closed captions, they can read what is being talked about in the video and either watch it through that way or save it to watch later when they can listen.

BE TRULY AUTHENTIC

One of my friends shared a great quote with me about being consistent: "Always make sure that your influence as it grows wide, that your character runs deep." What this is saying is that as your influence grows you need to make sure that your words and your actions are in 100% alignment. For example, if I'm on social media saying "this is what we do," then that needs to be backed up. People see authenticity, when they see your actions, following up with your words. When those two things meet consistently over time, not only will you attract the best talent to your team, you'll retain them, and people will actually lean into you. That quote is going to stick with me, and it's going to be something my team and I lean into in years to come.

BE THE LIGHTHOUSE

One of the greatest things a leader can do is be a lighthouse for others. People should be able to see you even in the darkness. To be a lighthouse for others, you have to be approachable and understanding. Make it known to your team that you have bad days too. When something doesn't go the right way, you have to respond in a positive way. How you respond to your setbacks, paves the way for how your team responds to setbacks. So ask yourself: How do you respond to setbacks? How do you respond to people not meeting their goals? And How do you bring people along on the journey without being the hammer? You have to focus on how to lift your team up and get them from A to B in a way that doesn't make you out to be the authoritative boss, but an influential mentor.

To be able to connect with someone and open the window to share and speak to them, you have to know who you are talking to. For example, let's say someone on your team isn't performing to their greatest potential in a certain area. You can start a dialogue with " I need to give you some tough love right now. Are you willing to accept what I'm going to share with you?" and most likely they will answer with a "yes." Then you have space to dive into the issue by saying something like "Here are some areas that you're winning in." and explain them. Then you could say "I believe you have greatness in this area, but we haven't figured out how to tap into it together. I need your help. We need to figure out how we can help you with this goal because I know you want to succeed. So, what do you think we could do?" This is a great example of an open dialogue that will create positive change.

Let's break that dialogue down, so you can apply it to your own scenarios. A leader should pull out the greatness in others, so first you should recognize the inherent greatness and capacity to do well. You should start with that, but don't shy away from the fact that they didn't reach the goal. Help them recognize that they didn't reach the goal, and then step in alongside them by asking what they need or what you can do to help them. This is what a great leader should be doing in their business because after that team member fixes the issue and achieves their goal, they will be able to help other people in the way that you helped them. It sets your business up for long-term success.

LEVERAGE THE STRENGTHS OF YOUR TEAM

If you or one of your team members is doing the work, but not getting the expected results it's okay to reach out to other leaders or members of your team because effort doesn't always equal results. You might be taking all the right steps, but still fall short. Something that modern leaders do well with is leveraging the strengths of their teams. Even though you're the leader of your team, that team member who is falling short might learn more from another team member than they could from you. Chances are each member of your team is going to have different strengths and weaknesses. Use those resources, and have your team learn from each other's strengths so that the leading doesn't all fall on you.

LEADING FROM THE FRONT

The modern leader is one that is a learner. You don't have to have all the answers to be a leader, but you have to be willing to learn. Leading from the front means that you are being an example for others, and showing them how to win and how to fail. You have to be vulnerable to be a great leader. You have to be willing to fail in front of your team because we learn more from our failures than our successes could ever teach us. This also means that if you are telling your team to do something that puts them out of their comfort zone, you better be first in line to go bungee jumping first. In other words, leading from the front means that you should never ask your team to do something that you wouldn't do or haven't already done yourself. If you show people how to get uncomfortable, they're going to have more confidence to get uncomfortable themselves.

TIPS YOU CAN USE TO DEVELOP YOUR TEAM

1. **Create a team motto or use this one.** In past years, my team had a motto: One more. For us, this phrase meant that we might not achieve all of our goals in a day, but before the day is over we can at least achieve one more. This meaning can actually reach outside the workplace. It can be for your health and wellness goals, getting one more burpee in, drinking one more glass of water, or reading one more chapter of a book. In my company, we used it as you can get one more call in today or one more loan. This has a huge impact individually, but when a whole team takes on this mentality you can achieve anything.

2. **Develop a new tactic for your team to grow.** A new tactic that my company had put into effect this year, is that everyone needs to get very clear on their beliefs and start doing their own videos. The company has provided great marketing as many companies do, but people want to hear from you. They want to hear from the actual humans that work within the company. So, the goal is to have everybody on our team to have at least one video that explains who they are and what they're passionate about. It's a big goal because that means that everyone is going to have to get vulnerable. The video could be a minute or three minutes. I don't really care how long it is, but I want everybody on our team to have the opportunity to see what happens when you put yourself out there and connect because in my experience the encouragement I received from

just being vulnerable and connecting helped me grow to where I am now.

3. **Get a coach, instead of just having mentors.** The fundamental difference between a mentor and a coach is that a coach is going to provide true accountability. That's the biggest difference because a mentor is not going to call you every day and see how your job is going. A mentor will give you wisdom and make you feel good, but it's only going to be a conversation. With a coach, they are going to make you get uncomfortable. The best coaches I've had have gotten me uncomfortable, and I'm glad they did because I learned so much through that space.

Want to hear the full conversation, head on over to https://www.thebriancoveyshow.com/

CHAPTER 11
COACH BURT

Coach Burt is considered "America's Coach," a unique blend of a former championship basketball coach combined with a deep methodology of inner-engineering people to produce at a higher level in the business world, or a coaching-preneur.

While talking with him, I was able to pull out some of his most valuable teachings, what makes a good coach, and what activating your prey drive really means. Here's what I learned in our conversation:

SHOW UP FOR THE BATTLE, WIN YOUR WAR

In the bible, King David was a great king, respected by all for his bravery and leadership. He went to war every year because he was the leader of many warriors, but the one year he decided to stay home, he went down a path of great mistakes. The year he stayed home is when he saw Bathsheba. That led him into deep trouble and sorrow because he wasn't supposed to be there. He was supposed to show up and fight with his warriors. When we decide to not show up for ourselves and our business, we run into troubles that never would have happened if we hadn't stayed home.

There are so many people who are choosing not to go into battle because the world might be changing and systems might not be the same as they always were, but that just means we have to adjust and work the system in a different way. The system is always going to be changing, but our drive should stay the same.

One of the core principles that Coach Burt lives by is to never allow another person to stand between you and your destiny. There's never a shortage of opportunity. An example of this is when Coach Burt's mother in law wanted to start making some extra money. She went to work delivering groceries for InstaCart. She found that some people were making $1,000 a week just for shopping and delivering groceries. Sounds pretty straight forward, right? It was and she made the extra money that she wanted. There are many simple jobs like this one and it goes to show that there is no shortage of jobs for people that want to show up and do the work. There's enough opportunity for you to become successful, but you have to get yourself out there and do the work.

The first time Coach Burt personally made $100,000, he joined a program. In this coaching program, he was in room "A" with people that were all making $100,000, and there was a room "B" with people that were making over a million in personal income per year. The coach of the program kept going back and forth between both rooms. He would teach Coach Burt's room for a little while and then he would go back to teach the other room. When he came back to Coach Burt's room, someone in the room raised their hand and asked "What's the difference between the people in the other room making a million dollars and the people in here making $100,000?" The coach didn't hesitate at all before explaining "That's simple. When I tell you guys to do something, you give me 10 reasons why it won't work, but when I tell them to do something, they just go do it." That is the difference between someone that makes 100,000 versus someone that makes a million dollars in personal income per year.

Now that we've discussed the importance of showing up, we can get into our conversation about coaching because the very first step in finding a great coach is making the conscious decision that you are going to show up for the battle and win your war.

WHAT YOU NEED TO KNOW BEFORE HIRING A BUSINESS COACH

A coach's job is to: Recruit and attract, coach and develop, & retain and optimize.

It's going to create sabotage if you go into a mentorship with the mindset that the coach is going to solve all your problems and make the magic happen for you. Their genius is to consult with you to guide you in the right direction. Think of coaching as engaging yourself in a set of behaviors. You don't do it just one time. You have to practice and make the behavior habit. For example, the military doesn't give a person an M16 rifle and tell them to just go watch a video. They teach them how to use it, develop their mindsets, and do enough practice to where hitting the target becomes a routine.

What happens when your routine gets thrown out the window? Now what? I asked Coach Burt how he is able to keep a routine even when things get shaky or fall out of order, and he made it very easy to understand… It's a simple decision. It's a simple decision to get wealthy or get in better shape, but it needs to be followed up by the simple decision to take consistent action. For a routine to become consistent, you have to build a conscience. If you start a workout routine and stick with it, you will start to feel guilty if you skip a workout. When you create healthy habits, you won't let yourself fall out of them. Even if something happens, maybe your gym closes for maintenance, you will still find a way to move that day because you've trained your body to crave the movement.

There's a new division of Coach Burt's company, a health assessment, called Monster Health that his wife is leading. There was a guy that set an ideal weight goal, and to reach that goal they told him he had to cut out the alcohol at night. Alcohol was one of the things that were giving him a big gut, but he didn't really know if he wanted to give it up because he liked having a drink at the end of the day. Coach Burt consoled him to get to his ideal weight first, and then you can have the alcohol, but you can't have the alcohol every night while you're trying to lose the weight. You have to choose which is more important to you. You have to ask yourself how badly do you want to lose weight? How tired are you of being broke? How embarrassed are you when someone is out there making 10 million a year and you're not? What do they have that you don't have? Nothing. You have the ability to make decisions for yourself. It's up to you to change your life.

DOING THE HARD WORK

You might think that finding a great coach to guide you in your career is all about what they do and how they show up for you, but it actually has more to do with how you show up for them. If you are meeting with a business coach, but you are not making the effort to do the work they're telling you to do, then your shortcomings are your fault and your fault alone. Your job is to take the coach's strategies, ideas, and advice to bring with you while you do the hard work.

Coach Burt had a business coach that he was paying about 400 an hour to coach him. In their very first meeting, the first thing the coach told him was that he had only one rule: you be all in, or you get out. The coach said to not come to him unprepared, or call him for small talk, but to show up ready to get coached. This coach and other coaches Coach Burt has had haven't sugar-coated anything. They were straight and to the point. That's the kind of coach to look for because they won't waste your time and they will call you out if you're wasting their time.

When you're in a coaching program, it is not the coach's job to make you be coached. It's your job to be coached and extract the full value of the relationship. The best way to make sure you are getting the most out of your coaching is to know what you want to gain before going into it. When Coach Burt was starting out, he went to a Tony Robbins 4-day coaching deal with a guy on his team. The price of the coaching event was $3,500 but within the first 15 minutes Coach Burt told his friend "Man, I got everything I need." What he wanted to gain was how does Tony Robbins get 10,000 people in a room.

Within those 15 minutes, he got his $3,500 worth of guidance. What Coach Burt has learned is that highly successful people are looking for one tactic, one strategy, or one idea, not to be entertained. Coach Burt was seeking coaching to learn strategies, ideas, and mindset but none of what he learned would have mattered if he didn't apply it. If you do the work on your end, a coaching program should result in going from 45 deals a year to 45 deals a month, as one of Coach Burt's clients did after applying Coach's strategies and ideas to his real estate business.

Success never happens by accident. It starts with showing up, working hard, and staying consistent to keep the muscles strong. When Coach Burt taught basketball he would tell his players to make no wasted movements. Every movement needed to have a purpose. From a pivot to a catch, to a drill, or defensive play there needed to be zero wasted movements. Every ounce of energy counted and had a purpose.

Now as a business coach, he sees tons of wasted movement because people get confused about what they're supposed to be doing, so they just stay where they are. It's a confusion of priority. Coach Burt debunked the theory of time management problems. He explained that the real problem people are having is actually a priority problem. If the number one purpose of any business is to create customers, which it should be, the priority needs to be to have a strategy, tactics, and an overall plan to do that. There needs to be some kind of growth system so that people don't find themselves wasting movements out of the confusion.

THE PREY DRIVE

We discussed how some people don't put their all in when working with a coach. They stay at the halfway point and don't dare to cross that middle line. Most people don't even think about their potential. They aren't having conversations about it or attempting to better themselves to a higher point. The average American is reading less than one book a year and not involved in any personal development programs or routines. Coach Burt explained that is the reason why a percentage of people dominate. Most people don't know what they don't know. They don't know what having a good coach, being a part of a great company, or being in the right environment can do. They just accept what their life is and that they are only ever going to make so much money.

At one point in Coach Burt's career, his wife questioned him about how much he works, and his response was that he was not going to live an ordinary life. He told her that he was going to live an extraordinary life, it wouldn't be normal, and that meant that he couldn't be normal. He wanted a private jet, a place in Florida, a million-dollar company, and to create long-term wealth. You can't give normal effort to achieve extraordinary results. He achieved all these things and more by showing up, working hard, and staying consistent. His prey drive is something that you can learn from and use in your own life or business.

During the pandemic, a friend of Coach Burt's made a billion dollars because he took a risk and had confidence. He figured out a way to buy masks from 3M, turn around and sell those masks, and he has a strong network. This friend failed in his business plans many times before, and he took a huge gamble on this latest plan, but it worked in his favor this time. He invested 10 million dollars, raised 74 million dollars in a matter of days, and in 90 days he made a billion dollars. The friend explained to Coach Burt that "He who hesitates, finishes last." The people that take action are the winners.

THE WHOLE PERSON THEORY

When Coach Burt began coaching people on business, he used what learned about The Whole Person Theory. The theory was nationalized by a man named Dr. Stephen Covey who wrote a book called *The Seven Habits* in 1989. Coach Burt read the book when he had just graduated from college at 19-years-old. The book explains how people are made up of four parts: a body, a mind, a heart, and a spirit. Each of these parts produces four different needs, bits of intelligence, capacities, and dimensions. The body represents skills, the mind represents knowledge, the heart represents desire, and the spirit represents confidence. The theory is if you're going to be a whole person and not a fragmented person, then you have to feed and nurture all four parts of your nature. Coach Burt grabbed this theory and decided he was going to use it to prescribe where a person needed coaching.

FROM COACHING TO THE BUSINESS WORLD

Coming from the athletic world to corporate America, Coach Burt brought the intensity that most businesses lack. As a basketball coach, he would be with the team from early in the morning until late at night practicing. They would watch films and show up on Saturdays. It was a lifestyle, and when Coach Burt brought that into the business world he was stunned at how low-intensity everyone was. Coach Burt read many books before going into the business world. The bank he made his first contract with wanted him to drive the largest retail initiative in the history of the bank, so he got his team to work. Within three months, the CEO of the bank called him and told him that he couldn't have his team working as hard as they were. They ended up showing a 43% increase that year.

From this work, Coach Burt noticed that the reason athletic coaches have more intensity than business professionals is that they always have something in front of them, a clear goal. Coaches have a championship to win or the next game to prepare for. If they lose, they have to make adjustments and have critical conversations. Then converting to the business world, Coach Burt noticed that they would let a person suck for six months before saying anything to them, not make any quick decisions and everyone went at a very comfortable pace. He realized that there needs to be a crossover between business and sports. There needs to be more strategy in coaching, and more intensity in business. With both strategy and intensity, you can be successful in any industry you choose to work in.

Want to hear the full conversation, head on over to https://www.thebriancoveyshow.com/

CHAPTER 12
BARRY HABIB

B arry Habib has had many successful businesses that he has founded, grown, and sold. This includes Mortgage Market Guide, Healthcare Imaging Solutions, and Certified Mortgage Associates. During Barry's mortgage sales career, he was recognized for having the highest annual origination production in the US on two occasions.

Barry personally originated over $2 Billion dollars in mortgage loan production over his career. He is also the Lead Producer and Managing Partner for *Rock of Ages*, a Broadway musical theatrical production, which was also released as a major film starring Tom Cruise. Barry also plays the part of the record producer in the movie. For over 20 years, Barry has been a well-known professional speaker in the financial and Real Estate markets.

In our talk, we discussed his background, his perception of success in America, and we walk through some key exercises to keep growing as an individual every day.

OPPORTUNITY INSPIRES HARD WORK

People that aren't from America or are here as a first-generation child will often hear a phrase be passed around that "there's money in the streets" in America. Other countries hear that America is so wealthy and rich. They hear that it is a country filled with opportunities for everyone and that anyone can be successful there. It's the American dream, going from rags to riches with good honest hard work mixed with ample opportunities.

Barry was an athlete in high school, and when he got to the college level, a lot of people passed him by even though he was really competitive and driven. He would get to practice early and practice late. He did extra work on his own. He wanted to be there, and he wanted it to be him that made it big in that sport. It just wasn't in the cards for him. He told me "God did not give me enough ability compared to the others that made the cut. So it wasn't there for me, but it wasn't for lack of trying." Athletics is a bit unfair. If you don't jump higher, run faster than someone else, it doesn't matter how much you try. There are physical advantages. But it's not like that for sales. In sales, I don't have to run faster than somebody, I don't have to jump higher, and I don't have to be stronger. All I need is one thing, and that is commitment. How much heart do you have? How much desire do you have? Do you want to push yourself to learn? Do you want to push yourself to be the best that there is? That's the beauty of business, you control your success, and nobody else.

Barry's parents were so curious about the money in the streets that they decided to venture out to America to see what they could accomplish here. We'll talk in more detail about Barry's parents later, but that's what drives every person to want to work hard, right? The opportunity. To put it in perspective, if every citizen automatically started off at a 50K per year salary when they turned 20-years-old, and knew that there would be no upward mobility in their careers, they wouldn't work harder because they have no opportunity. Opportunity inspires hard work, and what Barry found is that the money in the streets was only available to those who would be willing to work hard and do extra. The people that open their eyes to the opportunities that others pass by are the ones that pick up the money in the streets.

FINDING OPPORTUNITIES

People are extremely resistant to change, some more than others, but that's the only way to find opportunities. They can actually be small changes or tweaks. When Barry was learning how to fly, his instructor would tell him to make small changes because you can't make big shifts in the air or you'll lose control. It's the same thing in life. Sometimes big changes can be great if you are really on the wrong path, but most of the time smaller changes lead to greater outcomes. Making little tweaks in your day to day life can have a lasting effect on your success.

To become more open to change, you have to start with your mindset and how you approach every day. If you embrace change, you will start to see the opportunities. A lot of us think in the same way we drive. Barry mentioned that he has spent time with many driving instructors to become a better driver because he enjoys cars and track driving.

In his instructions, he was told that about 90% of people typically look directly at the car in front of them when they are driving, but they would be much better drivers if they stopped doing that. Instead, if you look down the road you'll see all the things that are happening instead of just what is right in front of you.

<u>Try This:</u>

- Take a bottle of water and put it about 15-20 feet in front of you on the ground.

- While looking at the bottle of water, focus on a sign or picture that is further away. You won't be able to see the sign or picture. But…

- If you focus your eyes on the sign or picture that is further away, you will still be able to see the bottle of water. Looking further away will allow you to see both, instead of just the bottle of water.

If you only focus on the bottle of water in front of you, you won't be able to see the other opportunities past it. In your own life, think about something that you've been focusing on. Maybe it's your job, your family, or your bills piling up. Whatever it is, if you try to look further ahead you will find that there are opportunities awaiting you. You might see a promotion, a better relationship with your family, or an idea that will boost your income. To find opportunities, you have to change your perspective and look further than the car in front of you.

Being Trustworthy

Every market is always going to be changing. The mortgage market was under fire only 20 months ago, and even though it is in a great place now we still need to be preparing for the future. The key to success in any sales is your ability to be able to convert from conversation to either application or contract. That's where you have to prepare. You have to start by winning people's trust and to do that you have to become trustworthy and knowledgeable in what you are selling. If you don't care enough about your product to know the ins and outs of it then no one else will care either. You have to know the advantages and disadvantages and be able to communicate those to buyers in a way that they feel comfortable trusting you. Your goal shouldn't be to sell the client but to really help them because you believe in what you're offering.

When Barry started selling stereo equipment as a young guy, in his early 20s, he devoured everything he could learn. He learned everything so that when he spoke to someone as a kid, he could gain their confidence right away as someone that really knew their stuff and was someone they could trust. Trust is what it's all about. Trust is what it's all about in a relationship, with your kids, with yourself, and with your customers.

Now, how do you win trust, and how do you do it quickly? There are two ways. The first is with your knowledge. Barry told me "you can't give what you don't have." This is where the money in the streets comes back into play. To be trusted, you have to have knowledge. To have the knowledge, it takes hard work. But here's the catch...the vast majority of people won't do it. That's why it's so great. That's why there is the saying of "money in the streets." It's so easy to be successful because many are not willing to do the extra work or even work at all. Do you know, great it feels when you're a master of your craft. It feels amazing because that confidence comes through and customers and business leaders start to recognize the hard work that sets you apart from others.

The other way that Barry explained is to become trusted by being completely transparent and telling people everything bad about the transaction. You won't hear this in many sales classes because it can be risky, especially if you have a product or service that is not beneficial. Which in that case, you should move to work with a different product anyway. Barry says to go out of your way to tell them everything bad. Show people that you're willing to lose a commission. Barry explained that "If it still benefits them, once you've crossed that enormous chasm, you are now able to win people's trust." and that goes for life as well. Be transparent and vulnerable in your relationships, with your kids, and with yourself. Don't be afraid.

You know that the bad stuff always comes up eventually, and if you are the salesperson that warns them about what could happen from the start, they will trust you and usually will be more willing to move forward with the transaction because they know you are not trying to trick them.

FEAR OF LOSS

It's really hard for salespeople to have a sale almost in the bag, and then lose it because they shy away from telling the customer about the risks. Most people know that you're going to start by telling them all the great features because it's our instinct to put our best foot forward. When you leave out the downside, and there is always a downside, your customers will think it is too good to be true and they will not buy. This is an "I got this commission, and I don't want to risk losing it" reaction, but then you end up losing it because you were too afraid to lose it.

In South America, a very rare animal to capture is spider monkeys and hunters who capture them have created a very ingenious way. Barry explained that because these monkeys are nocturnal, they only come out at night, they have these heavy boxes that are ventilated with the monkey's food that makes them go crazy. It is ventilated, so they can't get in, except for a small slit in the box. The monkeys are smart, they find it at night, there's no one around, they get the slit in the box, they put their hand in, they get the food, but when they go to take their food out, they can't get it out because the clenched fist can't get out of the box.

All the monkey has to do to get its freedom and everything they want is let go. But because they don't let go, they essentially trap and capture themselves. Then the hunters just come and pick them up. What we need to understand is that by trying to be overly protective, we trap ourselves.

For instance, how did your relationship work out when you were all over someone and not letting them breathe? Have you experienced a similar situation with your customer? The needier you are to your client, the more desperate you appear.

People who are desperate will do or say anything, whether or not it's in the best interest of the customer. The more you show that customer that you can stand back the better chance at selling you will have. Instead of being on opposite ends of the table, be on the same side of the table, and essentially treat that customer as if it were your child, your parent, your best friend, and warn them of things instead of selling them on things. That makes all the difference in the world. Then who else are they going to go with? That that transcends price? They are going to only be willing to do business with you and then tell everyone they know about how truthful and knowledgeable you are about said product or service.

HOW TO STAY AHEAD

A trick to staying ahead is to become magnetic. Barry explained how to do this.

Try This:

1. Everyone you come into contact with, try to help them be better or feel better. If you do that, they'll want more of that. By definition, they will be drawn to you like a magnet. You can't give what you don't have which means you have to put in the work and prior to that so you have something to give to allow them to feel better.

2. The other thing that makes people very magnetic is confidence, not cockiness. Now, how do you gain confidence? Confidence comes from being the absolute best version of yourself, right now. Think about that. Are you having your best week? month? Year? Are you doing

better now, given the circumstances you have than you would have done a month ago, a week ago? Are you growing? That's what gives you confidence. Knowing that I've never been better than I am right now, gives you confidence that just shines through. People are drawn to that. They want to be close to you, work with you, and learn from you.

We're in a wonderful age. Barry told me "20 years ago, you couldn't do a show like you're doing right now Brian." He told me that because I'm getting out there with a lot of credible people, I'm becoming more familiar now. That familiarity really helps in building trust. You become a brand. When you go to the supermarket and you see an item there, that's a brand that you recognize, so you tend to gravitate towards those, you know. There is a specific reason for this, it is a survival mechanism that's been ingrained in our minds. We recognize patterns that are familiar to us and make us feel safer. That's why, if you are in any kind of sales, it is really important for your brand to be out there, utilizing the beauty and no cost of social media.

You can't just get out there and say, "Hey, come to me," you have to provide value. Barry said "You're trying to bring on guests that may provide value, and it's a privilege for me to be with you here. You're helping others." When Barry first got into the mortgage business, he had to learn everything, to be an advisor, an expert. By putting in all of that time it allowed him as a young kid in the mortgage business to win the trust of people that were decades older than him, who had much more experience than him.

Barry is an excellent example of an impeccable business-man who still to this day strives to keep being successful in his career by being an expert in his field, learning every day because there's so much to learn. This allows him to stay ahead. When we utilize things like social media and put ourselves out there to people, it changes everything. Then people start to view you as that resource, that authority, that familiar brand, that they know that they can trust. So, build your brand, make yourself familiar, and keep learning every single day to be an expert in your field and to stay ahead.

WHAT DRIVES YOU?

When I asked Barry what drives him to keep learning and growing even though he has already achieved such a high level of greatness, he said that he demands it of himself because it gives him fulfillment. He said "My parents made an unbelievable sacrifice, to allow me to have opportunity and God gave me talents. I'm not gonna let them down. I'm not going to let my kids down. I'm not going to set an example for my kids, showing them it's okay to put it on cruise control. I want them to see that the right thing to do is to push yourself and to demand yourself to be the very best you can." If you want to stay inspired to keep learning and growing, find what drives you. Do you have a reason to keep being better than you were yesterday? What is it? Use that reason to keep driving yourself to be better every day.

BARRY'S BACKGROUND

Barry's parents were immigrants from Europe and they thought the United States was filled with great opportunity. When they arrived, they found that it was a lot tougher than they expected, especially not speaking the language. His dad was an international journalist who spoke 10 languages, and his mother spoke 7 languages but was pulled out of school at a very young age and although extremely intelligent, she never learned to read or write. Barry's father died when he was a kid, and his mother didn't make much money due to her lack of career options, but she would always tell him the stories she heard before they came to America about there being money in the streets. After learning and growing, Barry was able to sit with his mom before she passed away and tell her "Mom, you were right. There really is money in the streets here." He found that all you have to be able to do is see it, be able to pick it up and do good with it. All of us are trying to figure out where the money in the streets is and what unique opportunities are out there for us.

Want to hear the full conversation, head on over to https://www.thebriancoveyshow.com/

FINAL NOTE

Dear Reader,

We are always learning and growing on the Brian Covey show, so I hope you will listen to the rest of the life-changing podcasts either through my website, briancovey.com.

If you gained nothing else throughout the course of this book but these 5 things, then it was more than worth it to bring it to you because these 5 things are the basics to building the life you've always wanted. The 5 basic tenants that I learned from the advice of the extraordinary people in this book are to...

1. Be kind to others

2. Always be addicted to growth through personal development

3. Share your talents with others

4. Surround yourself with great people

5. Be passionate about your vision

I think that there are bigger possibilities within you to create a life that aligns up with who you are and what your dreams are. By taking small steps consistently, in that right direction, you'll be able to achieve it. Not one person highlighted in this book was an overnight success. It was a process to get to where we are, and that process is a lifelong journey with ample opportunities to continue to learn and grow, committing to that process.

To me, it's more important about who you're becoming, than your past or who you are today. Where do you want to see your future self? Really think about that. Then take a step back and pinpoint what those steps and building blocks are to get there. Now, get out there and do the work to win your game of life.

With Encouragement,

Brian Covey

ABOUT THE AUTHOR

Once an Olympic USA Soccer Player, Brian quickly learned how to leverage the right mindset on and off the field. Fitness and mindset became masteries for Brian very early as his career was affected by the 2007 market crash just years after his soccer team days came to an end, right when he was raising toddlers with his wife Nicole. Brian has mastered the art of a growth mindset, the art of winning, and the art of staying fit. He believes in integration, hard work & consistency. Brian is an executive at loanDepot, a proud father, an influencer, a top-rated podcaster and, just simply, a fabulous soccer dad.

Brian believes a few simple things:

1. Be kind to others and put out positive energy to attract the right people

2. Always be a learner and addicted to growth through personal development

3. Be hungry and have hustle in your game, giving, & sharing of your talents and gifts with others

4. Surround yourself with great people - association matters

5. Be passionate about your vision and live your purpose today

If this resonates with you, connect with Brian on his social channels and podcasts.

Made in the USA
Middletown, DE
28 November 2021

53283387R00056